Sacré-Cœur

Montmartre

Pussy cat's tour of Paris

Musée du Louvre
(Louvre Museum)

Le Centre Pompidou
(Pompidou Centre)

Pont Neuf

Cathédrale
Notre-Dame de Paris
(Notre-Dame Cathedral)

Place de la Bastille

Pussy cat, pussy cat, where have you been?

I've been to Paris, and guess what I've seen...

Russell Punter

Illustrated by Dan Taylor

Pussy cat, pussy cat,
where have you been?

I've been to Paris,
and guess what I've seen...

I cruised down the Seine, where the bridges are pretty.
Pont Neuf is the oldest in all of the city.

I saw Notre-Dame, a cathedral nearby.
Creepy stone gargoyles look down from on high.

Paris is packed with patisserie shops,
selling pastries and gateaux, with chocolate on top.

"A prison once stood at Bastille," said a guide.
"The King kept his enemies locked up inside."

At the Pompidou Centre, pipes cover the walls,

while great modern art can be found in its halls.

Close to the Seine is the Louvre Museum.
Its paintings are famous, so I went to see them.

The entrance alone is a wonderful sight.
The stunning glass pyramids glint in the light.

Inside there are sculptures and artworks galore.
I followed a guide who was giving a tour.

"Here is a painting you simply must see, sir.
A world-famous portrait – she's called Mona Lisa."

At the grand Opera House, you can hear people sing.

Its breathtaking hallways are fit for a king.

Sacré-Cœur is a church at the top of a hill.
I went up by railway – the ride is a thrill.

On the streets of Montmartre, I stopped in a square.
My portrait was drawn as I posed on a chair.

If you want to see more, then the train is a treat.
It chugs over cobbles and winds through the streets.

The huge Arc de Triomphe has sculptures that show
French soldiers in battle from days long ago.

The long Champs-Élysées is bordered by trees.
I stopped at a café for French bread and cheese.

The Tour de France racers come here in July.
In a sprint to the finish, the riders fly by.

I hired a bike, and explored for an hour,
then cycled along to the tall Eiffel Tower.

The view from the top is a wonderful scene.
I looked across Paris, at where I had been.

I was joined by some people I'd seen on my stay,
and we promised ourselves that we'd come back one day.

So do visit Paris, if you get the chance.
"Vive la France," as the French say,
which means, "Long live France!"

Edited by Lesley Sims

First published in 2017 by Usborne Publishing Ltd., Usborne House, 83-85 Saffron Hill,
London EC1N 8RT, England. www.usborne.com Copyright © 2017 Usborne Publishing Ltd.

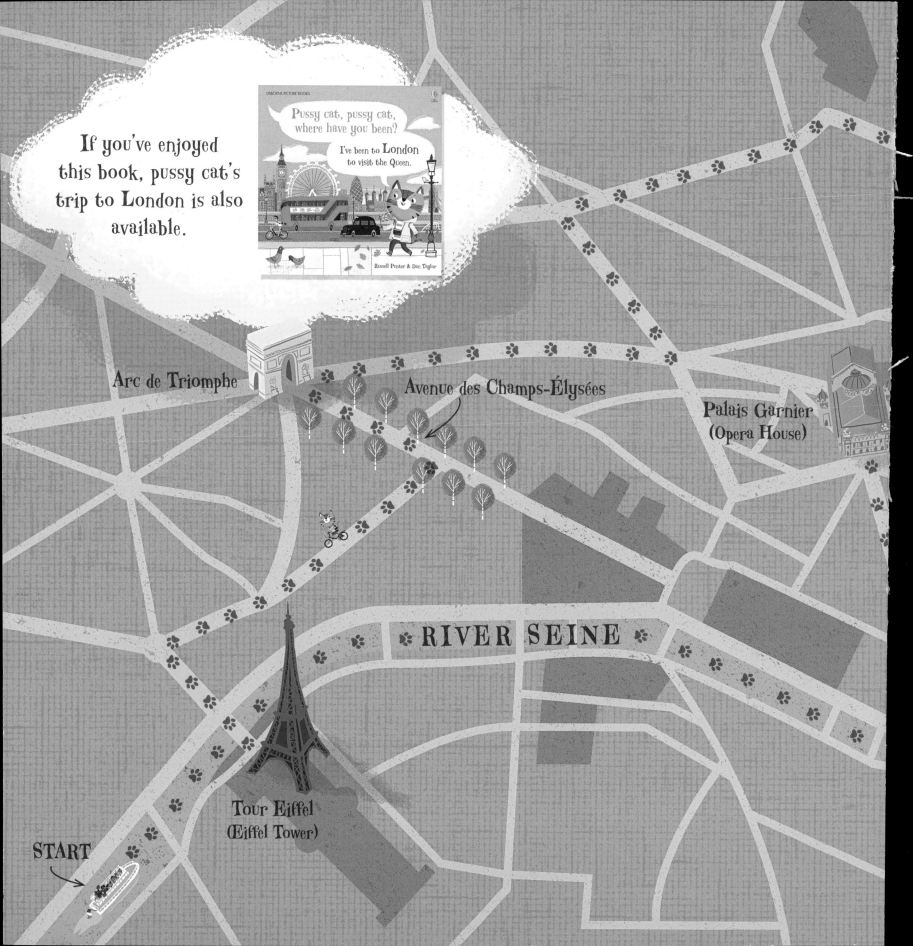

If you've enjoyed this book, pussy cat's trip to London is also available.

Pussy cat, pussy cat, where have you been?

I've been to London to visit the Queen.

Russell Punter & Dan Taylor

Arc de Triomphe

Avenue des Champs-Élysées

Palais Garnier
(Opera House)

RIVER SEINE

Tour Eiffel
(Eiffel Tower)

START